Handbook for Chaplains

Comfort My People

"Comfort, comfort my people, says your God."
(Isaiah 40:1)

Mary M. Toole

New York/Ma...

Cover and book design by Lynn Else

Library of Congress Cataloging-in-Publication Data

Toole, Mary M.
    Handbook for chaplains : comfort my people / Mary M. Toole.
      p. cm.
    "Comfort, comfort my people, says your God" (Isaiah 40:1).
    Includes bibliographical references.
    ISBN 0-8091-4386-0 (alk. paper)
    1. Chaplains—Handbooks, manuals, etc. 2. Religions. 3. Prayers.
I. Title.
    BV4375.T66 2006
    253—dc22

                        2005032900

Published by Paulist Press
997 Macarthur Boulevard
Mahwah, New Jersey 07430

www.paulistpress.com

Printed and bound in the United States of America

Contents

Appreciations

Special thanks go to the following people for sharing their knowledge with me: Fr. Tom (Msgr. Thomas Hartman) of the God Squad, coauthor of *Religion for Dummies*; Dr. Faroque Khan who wrote, in the *Fordham Urban Law Journal*, "Religious Teachings on Advance Directive-Religious Values and Legal Dilemmas in Bioethics: An Islamic Perspective"; Surabhi Splain for her help in my learning about Buddhist and Hindu traditions; and David Snyder for proofing and editing the section on Judaism.

Acknowledgments

The Publisher gratefully acknowledges use of the following: Father Mychal Judge, OFM, Holy Name Province, Order of Friars Minor—Franciscan Friars. New York. Prayer used with permission. Francesca Fremantle and Chogyam Trungpa, *Tibetan Book of the Dead*, prayers used with permission of Shambhala. Excerpts from *Occasional Services: A Companion to Lutheran Book of Worship*, used with permission of Augsburg Fortress. Holy Bible, New Living Translation, used with permission of Tyndale House Publishers, Inc. All rights reserved. http://1stholistic.com/Spl_prayers/prayers_maha-mantra.htm. International Cyber Business Services, Inc. Prayers used with permission. Rabbi Marc Gellman and Msgr. Thomas Hartman, *Religion for Dummies*, excerpts reprinted with permission of Wiley Publishing Inc., a subsidiary of John Wiley & Sons, Inc. Michael Lotker, *A Christian's Guide to Judaism*, excerpts used with permission of Paulist Press. Abdullah Yusuf Ali, *The Meaning of the Holy Qur'ān*, excerpts used with permission of Amana Publications. *Summarized—Sahih-Al Bukhan Hadith*, excerpts used with permission of Dar-us-Salem Publisher. Reproductions from *The Complete Art Scroll Siddur*, edited by Rabbi Nosson Scherman and Rabbi Meir Zlotowitz, with permission from copyright holders: Artscroll/Mesorah Publications,

Opening Prayer

Lord, take me where You want me to go;
Let me meet who You want me to meet;
Tell me what You want me to say; and
Keep me out of your way.[1]

—*Father Mychal Judge*

Buddhism

Beliefs

Buddhists search for the Enlightenment (Nirvana), which is knowing what is true about the universe: that everyone shares the same Buddha nature. There are four noble truths: life is full of suffering; suffering comes from greed, hatred, and ignorance; there can be an end to suffering; and that comes from following the Eightfold Path. The Eightfold Path includes: (1) to have the highest view of the oneness of things in their pure nature; (2) to have the right thoughts of love and non-violence; (3) to use our speech in the right way; (4) to perform the right actions (peaceful and moral); (5) to perform the right kind of work or livelihood; (6) to act with discipline and right effort; (7) to be mindful in all our actions; and (8) to concentrate and meditate in the right way.

Birth

Buddhists celebrate many rituals from birth to adolescence. The first ceremony begins with the pregnancy, with another ceremony performed during labor. Other ceremonies include head washing several days after birth, a cradle ceremony as the baby is placed in a new cradle, and a naming ceremony. Girls have an ear-piercing ceremony and boys have a hair-tying ceremony.

Diet

Most Buddhists are vegetarians.

Sickness

According to the Buddhist teachings, all life is sacred and one should avoid destroying life. Life-support measures and resuscitation may be used. For the Buddhist, it is important to die with a positive state of mind. If living even for a few minutes longer will allow the person to have positive, virtuous thoughts, then they should be allowed this time. When life-support mechanisms provide no hope, it is permissible to remove the equipment. Some medical actions, such as resuscitation, can be violent and disturbing to the peace of the dying person. It is important for the dying person to die in a peaceful atmosphere.

Since pain medication may affect the alertness of the mind as well as ease pain, a Buddhist may refuse pain medication. The Buddhist may be working on achieving a positive state of mind, and this request by the patient should be honored.

Organ donation is permitted. It is considered an extremely positive act, coming from the compassionate desire to benefit others.

Dying/Death

When someone is dying, those ministering to them should try to give them hope and help them find forgiveness. It is normal for people who are dying to have regrets, guilt, and resentments. Listen as they share. When appropriate, remind them what they have accomplished and what they have done well. Help them to die in a peaceful frame of mind by encouraging them to forgive people and events in their life.

Be there for the person. Look into the person's eyes, touch his or her hands, or breathe with the same rhythm. It is not always necessary to say or do something.

The position for dying is to lie on the right side. The left hand rests on the left thigh. The legs are stretched out, and only gently bent. There are no special preparations for the body. Normal hospital procedures are satisfactory.

To avoid disturbing the consciousness during transition from death to a new life, the person's body should be left alone for as long as possible after death. Cremation will occur three to five days after the death. A memorial eulogy may be conducted using some readings from a Buddhist scripture, such as the following:

Prayers

For Contentment

By the power and the truth of this practice, may all beings have happiness, and the causes of happiness. May all be free from sorrow, and the causes of sorrow. May all never be separated from the sacred happiness, which is sorrowless. And may all live in equanimity, without too much attachment and too much aversion, and live believing in the equality of all that lives.

Prayer for a Person at Death

O son/daughter of an enlightened family, what is called death has now arrived, so adopt this attitude: "I have arrived at the time of death, so now, by means of this death, I will adopt only the attitude of the enlightened state of mind, loving kindness and compassion, and attain perfect enlightenment for the sake of all sentient beings who are as limitless as space."[2]

Chant

Om mani Padme Hum (invoking the Buddha who is the jewel of the Lotus into our heart).

Christianity

Beliefs

The word *Christian* is an umbrella name for all who believe in Jesus Christ as the Son of God, the Messiah, who died on the cross to redeem the world and rose to heaven. Jesus taught that God is love, and that love is the greatest commandment.

The first permanent split within the Christian religion occurred in 1054 when Christianity became divided into a Roman Church in the West and an Orthodox Church in the East. At the time, the Christians in the East followed the patriarch in Constantinople, known today as Istanbul. Priests of the Orthodox faith can marry, if they do not become bishops, and communion is in the form of real leavened bread, but usually in the form of an unleavened wafer in the West. The Christians in the West are under the guidance and jurisdiction of the Bishop of Rome, the pope, and priests under the Latin rite may never marry. Today, both Eastern and Western churches pray in the language of the people.

Protestants broke from the Western church beginning with Martin Luther (Lutherans). This group of people believed only God could forgive sins, and the only sacraments were Baptism and Holy Communion. They did not see the necessity of a pope, and priests were allowed to marry. Other Protestant denominations that emerged include: Calvinists, Presbyterians, Methodists, Baptists, Episcopalians, Congregationalists, Seventh Day Adventists, and Pentecostalists. Variations involve the role of a bishop, having women priests, reading the Bible more, and the use of music during services. Protestants wanted a say in how their church operated.

Birth

Baptism is regarded as a sacrament by some Christian religions, and signifies the initiation of a person as a Christian. Roman Catholics, Lutherans, and Episcopalians are encouraged to be baptized as an infant. Other Christian religions believe the person must be old enough to understand the sacrament or have the need to be "saved" before being baptized.

When a person is in danger of death, a priest, minister, chaplain, or any available Christian may perform a baptism. In the case of a child, this should be done with the consent of the parents. Water should be poured on the person while saying the words: "I baptize you (name of person) in the name of the Father, and of the Son, and of the Holy Spirit. Amen." However, in the case of an Orthodox person, only a priest or minister may baptize. If an Orthodox priest is not available and a baptism takes place, an Orthodox priest is to be informed after the baptism.

Diet

Most Protestant religions do not have a fasting requirement.

Roman Catholics are required to fast and abstain from meat on Ash Wednesday, Good Friday, all Fridays of Lent, and to fast for an hour before receiving the Eucharist. However, fasting rules are not enforced during illness.

People of the Orthodox faith must fast from meat and animal products, including eggs, milk, cheese, and butter on Wednesdays and Fridays, the Great Lent, and at other designated times.

Seventh Day Adventists do not allow the use of tobacco or alcohol.

Members of the Church of Latter Day Saints avoid alcohol, tea, coffee, tobacco, and cola drinks, and are encouraged to eat meat sparingly.

Sickness

All Christian religions require respect and dignity for the human body.

Organ donations and autopsies are allowed. When treatment for an illness is providing no reasonable benefit or is an unreasonable burden, it is acceptable to forego the treatment, allowing the dying process to proceed naturally. Decisions rest with the individual consciences of the patient and family.

Dying/Death

All Christian religions are open to pastoral care and uphold the dignity of the human body. During a loved one's final days, a few Christian churches have a rite of anointing. Only a priest may perform this rite. The person receiving the anointing may receive it more than once. After death has occurred, the rite may not be performed, although the Orthodox religion will permit anointing shortly after death has occurred.

Prayers

A Christian Prayer for Healing

Merciful Lord God, constant source of all healing, we give you thanks for all your gifts of strength and life, and above all we thank you for the gift of your Son, through whom we have health and salvation. As we wait for that day when there will be no more pain, help us by your Holy Spirit to be assured of your power in our lives and to trust in your eternal love; through Jesus Christ our Lord. Amen.[3]

Psalm 23

The LORD is my shepherd, I shall not be in want.
He makes me lie down in green pastures,

he leads me beside quiet waters,
   he restores my soul.
He guides me in paths of righteousness
   for his name's sake.
Even though I walk
through the valley of the shadow of death,
   I will fear no evil,
   for you are with me;
   your rod and your staff,
   they comfort me.
You prepare a table before me
   in the presence of my enemies.
   You anoint my head with oil;
   my cup overflows.
Surely goodness and love will follow me
   all the days of my life,
   and I will dwell in the house of the LORD forever.

Psalm 23 (Contemporary Version)[4]

The Lord is my Shepherd	That's Relationship!
I shall not want	That's Supply!
He maketh me to lie down in green pastures	That's Rest!
He leadeth me beside the still waters	That's Refreshment!
He restoreth my soul	That's Healing!
He leadeth me in the paths of righteousness	That's Guidance!
For His name's sake	That's Purpose!

Yea, though I walk through the valley of the shadow of death	That's Testing!
I will fear no evil	That's Protection!
For Thou art with me	That's Discipline!
Thou preparest a table before me in the presence of mine enemies	That's Hope!
Thou anointest my head with oil	That's Consecration!
My cup runneth over	That's Abundance!
Surely goodness and mercy shall follow me all the days of my life	That's Blessing!
And I will dwell in the house of the Lord	That's Security!
Forever	That's Eternity!

Psalm 25

To you, O LORD, I lift up my soul;
in you I trust, O my God.
    Do not let me be put to shame,
      nor let my enemies triumph over me.
No one whose hope is in you
    will ever be put to shame,
    but they will be put to shame
    who are treacherous without excuse.
Show me your ways, O LORD,
    teach me your paths;

guide me in your truth and teach me,
  for you are God my Savior,
  and my hope is in you all day long.
Remember, O LORD, your great mercy and love,
  for they are from of old.
Remember not the sins of my youth
  and my rebellious ways;
  according to your love remember me,
  for you are good, O LORD.
Good and upright is the LORD;
  therefore he instructs sinners in his ways.
He guides the humble in what is right
  and teaches them his way.
All the ways of the LORD are loving and faithful
  for those who keep the demands of his covenant.
For the sake of your name, O LORD,
  forgive my iniquity, though it is great.
Who, then, is the man that fears the LORD?
  He will instruct him in the way chosen for him.
He will spend his days in prosperity,
  and his descendants will inherit the land.
The LORD confides in those who fear him;
  he makes his covenant known to them.
My eyes are ever on the LORD,
  for only he will release my feet from the snare.
Turn to me and be gracious to me,
  for I am lonely and afflicted.
The troubles of my heart have multiplied;
  free me from my anguish.

Look upon my affliction and my distress
   and take away all my sins.
See how my enemies have increased
   and how fiercely they hate me!
Guard my life and rescue me;
   let me not be put to shame,
   for I take refuge in you.
May integrity and uprightness protect me,
   because my hope is in you.
Redeem Israel, O God,
   from all their troubles!

Psalm 130

Out of the depths I cry to you, O LORD;
O Lord, hear my voice.
   Let your ears be attentive
   to my cry for mercy.
If you, O LORD, kept a record of sins,
   O Lord, who could stand?
But with you there is forgiveness;
   therefore you are feared.
I wait for the LORD, my soul waits,
   and in his word I put my hope.
My soul waits for the Lord
   more than watchmen wait for the morning,
   more than watchmen wait for the morning.
O Israel, put your hope in the LORD,
   for with the LORD is unfailing love
   and with him is full redemption.

He himself will redeem Israel
from all their sins.

Prayer of Praise
(Canticle of Brother Sun and Sister Moon)

Most High, all-powerful, all-good Lord, all praise is Yours, all glory, all honor and all blessings. To you alone, Most High, do they belong, and no mortal lips are worthy to pronounce Your Name.

Praised be You my Lord with all Your creatures, especially Sir Brother Sun, Who is the day through whom You give us light. And he is beautiful and radiant with great splendor, of You Most High, he bears the likeness.

Praised be You, my Lord, through Sister Moon and the stars, in the heavens you have made them bright, precious, and fair.

Praised be You, my Lord, through Brother Wind and Air, and fair and stormy, all weather's moods, by which You cherish all that You have made.

Praised be You my Lord through Sister Water, so useful, humble, precious and pure.

Praised be You my Lord through Brother Fire, through whom You light the night and he is beautiful and playful and robust and strong.

Praised be You my Lord through our Sister, Mother Earth who sustains and governs us, producing varied fruits with colored flowers and herbs. Praised be

You my Lord through those who grant pardon for love of You and bear sickness and trial. Blessed are those who endure in peace, by You Most High.

Praised be You, my Lord through Sister Death, from whom no-one living can escape. Woe to those who die in mortal sin! Blessed are they She finds doing Your Will. No second death can do them harm. Praise and bless my Lord and give Him thanks, And serve Him with great humility.[5]

—*Saint Francis of Assisi*

Hinduism

Beliefs

Religion is a way of life, not separate from everyday life. Hindu beliefs include the existence of a soul; the reincarnation of the soul going through many births until enlightenment has been attained *(moksha)*; good actions, thoughts, and words that bring good karma and happiness. A Hindu is concerned with realizing the true Self. Their scripture *(Vedas)* suggests three ways to obtain self-realization: listening *(sravanam)*, thinking or remembering *(mananam)*, and concentration and meditation on self *(nidhidhyasana)*. There are five obligations for all Hindus: to worship daily, to participate in Hindu festivals, to live a life of duty and good conduct (thinking of others first), to observe the many sacraments marking passages of life, and to make a pilgrimage each year to holy people/temples near or far away.

Birth

There are rites, called *samskars*, associated with the birth of a child, the goal being to create an atmosphere to maintain a virtuous life. Some of these rites are:

garbhadana (conception)—prayer to conceive a child, an obligation in order to continue the human race; *punsavana* (fetus protection)—performed in the third or fourth month of pregnancy invoking divine qualities for the child; *simantonnayana* (satisfying the craving of the pregnant mother)—occurs during the seventh month of the pregnancy. Additional *samskars* include: *jatakarna* (childbirth)—which welcomes the child into the family with mantras for a long and healthy life; *namakarma* (naming the child)—which occurs four months after birth, when the child will be named after saints, sages, or holy people; and *annaprasana* (giving the child first solid food)—performed seven to eight months after birth.

Diet

Hindus tend not to eat meat, fish, or eggs.

Sickness

Close family members will be with a patient during an illness, assuming daily care of the loved one (i.e., washing, feeding, etc.). The father or eldest son makes all decisions regarding the health care of a loved one, but will include a family discussion. Modesty is important to a Hindu, so the sick person will prefer a same-sex caregiver.

Hindus are very stoic when it comes to pain. However, a woman may moan and groan during the delivery of a child.

Dying/Death

Terminal diagnosis is given to a family member and not the patient. The family will then decide how much or how little of the information will be shared with the patient.

It is better if, prior to an illness, families have discussed how much should be shared and with whom to share the information.

Death for Hindus signifies the passage from one life to their next life, which is determined by how they lived the life that just ended. The body will be washed, usually by the eldest son, and then cremated.

Prayers

As a greeting, Hindus join hands at the palms and bow from the waist and say *Namaskar* or *Namaste*, which means "I bow to God in you; I love you and I respect you, as there is no one like you."

A mantra is a sacred word. Uttering a mantra puts one in a special relationship with God. The most common mantra is the syllable *OM*.

Prayer Said When Greeting a Patient

Jai Shree Krishna.

The *Maha Mrityunjaya* Mantra

(Used for protection from accidents and daily mishaps in a busy life.)

Threyambakam yajaamahe sugandhim pushti-vardhanam. Oorvaarukamiva bandhanaath mrityor mikshieya maamamruthaath.[6]

Meaning

I worship the three-eyed Lord who is naturally fragrant, immensely merciful, and who is the Protector of the devotees. By your Grace, Let me be in the state of salvation (*moksha*) and be saved from the clutches of fearful death.

Gayatri Mantra — to the Lord Sun in the Cosmos

O God, The Giver of Life,
Remover of pains and sorrows,
Bestower of happiness, and
Creator of the Universe;
Thou art luminous, pure and adorable;
We meditate on Thee;
May Thou inspire and guide
Our intellect in the right direction.[7]

Brief Vedic Prayer (for all aspects of life)

O! All powerful God. You art the protector of the whole physical creation. May You protect my body. You art the source of all life. You art the source of all strength. May thou make me strong. O, omnipotent Lord, I live to thee to fill up all my wants and to give me perfection, physical, mental and spiritual.[8]

Morning Prayer

May all in this world be happy. May they be healthy. May they be comfortable and never miserable.

May the rain come down in the proper time. May the earth yield plenty of corn. May the country be free from war. May the Brahmans be secure.[9]

Prayers from *Yajur Veda*

O Thou glorious Lord, O Protector of vows, I am determined to master my lower self. Bestow on me the required strength and make my effort fruitful. Through Thy grace, leaving untruth, may I realize the Truth.

I worship You, O sweet Lord of transcendental vision, O Giver of prosperity to all! May I be free from bonds of death, like the ripe fruit falling from the tree. May I never again forget my immortal nature.

O Lord! Who blesses all creatures by revealing the Vedas, design to make us happy by Your calm and blissful self, which roots out terror as well as sin.

Salutations to Thee! O Destroyer of the cycle of births and deaths. O Lord of the universe, salutations to Thee.

O Lord! You art beyond the sea of *samsara* (ignorance). You existeth in its midst also. You enableth one to go beyond sin by means of the sacred mantras (chants). You taketh one beyond death through knowledge. I bow to Thee. Thou art present in sacred flowing streams as well as on the coastland. Thou art in the tender grass on the sea shore as well as in the foaming waves; I bow to Thee.

May I be able to look upon all creatures, with the eye of a friend. May we look upon one another with the eye of a friend.

O Lord!
Thou art infinite energy. Do fill me with energy.
Thou art infinite virility. Do fill me with virility.
Thou art infinite strength. Do grant us power.

Thou art infinite courage. Do make me courageous.
Thou art infinite fortitude. Do fill me with fortitude.

O Lord thou art our father. Do You instruct us like a
father. Our prostrations unto thee. Do not forsake us.
Do Thou protect us forever.

May we meet together, talk together, let our minds
apprehend alike; common be our prayer; common be
our assembly's aim; common be our purposes; common be our deliberation; common be our desires;
united be our hearts; united be our intention; so that
there may be a thorough union among all of us. May
our father grant this.

Let us meditate on the glory and splendor of our
Supreme Being, who illumines everything. May He
guide us in all our actions. May He grant us a clear
understanding and a pure intellect.[10]

—From *Yajur Veda*

Prayer by *Santideva*

As no one desires the slightest suffering nor ever has
enough of happiness, there is no difference between
myself and others, so let me make others joyfully
happy.

May those feeble with cold find warmth, and may those oppressed with heat be cooled by the boundless waters that pour forth from the great clouds of the Bodhisattvas.

May the rains of lava, blazing stones and weapons from now on become a rain of flowers, and may all battling with weapons from now on be a playful exchange of flowers.

May the naked find clothing, the hungry find food; may the thirsty find water and delicious drinks.

May the frightened cease to be afraid and those bound be freed; may the powerless find power, and may people think of benefiting one another.

For as long as space endures and for as long as living beings remain, until then may I too abide to dispel the misery of the world.[11]

Where the Mind Is Without Fear

Where the mind is without fear and the head is held high; Where knowledge is free; Where the world has not been broken up into fragments by narrow domestic wars; Where words come out from the depth of truth; Where tireless striving stretches its arms towards perfection; Where the clear stream of reason has not lost its way into the dreary desert sand of dead habit; Where the mind is led forward by thee into ever-widening thought and action—Into that heaven of freedom, my Father, let my country awake.[12]

Islam

Beliefs

Islam means the submission or surrender of one's will to the only true god, *Allah*. Anyone who does so is termed a *Muslim*. There is only one God who created everything and sustains everything. For Muslims, there will be a last day and a resurrection. On the last day, each will be judged. Those who did not follow God's call to mercy and goodness will go to hell. Those who did try to follow God's call to mercy and goodness will be rewarded with heaven and paradise.

There are five ways, called the *Five Pillars of Faith*, that Muslims follow God's call to mercy and goodness. The first and most important pillar of Islam is to pray the testimony of faith, the *Shahadah:* "There is no god but God, and Muhammad is his prophet."[13] They are to pray five times a day; they are to support the needy by *zakat* (almsgiving)—giving a specified percentage on certain properties—which is distributed to people in need; they are to fast each year throughout the month of Ramadan when there is no eating, drinking, smoking, or sexual relations from dawn to sunset; and if financially and physically capable, they are to make a pilgrimage to Mecca once in their lifetime.

Birth

Before a Muslim couple makes love, they pray the *Bismillah*, "in the Name of God, the Merciful, the Compassionate."[14] When a child is born, the parents pray into the baby's ear the *adhan*, the *Allahu Akbar* (call to prayer) and the *Shahadah*. Honey is placed on the baby's lips to make the child sweet and kind.

Circumcision is prescribed for a male baby and may be done at any time. A ceremony is not required. Most Muslims will want the baby boy circumcised before leaving the hospital. Circumcision is done for the purpose of facilitating cleanliness.

Muslim women will most likely breast-feed their child for a period of up to two years after birth.

Diet

Muslims may not eat pork or its by-products. This includes not eating anything that contains lard, gelatin, or pork products.

Sickness

A Muslim may pray five times a day, even when hospitalized. Before praying, the patient will clean his/her body, clothing, and the area for prayer of any bodily waste. The patient will wash his/her hands, forearms, mouth and nostrils, and face, wiping the top of the head, the ears, and the feet. If the patient is not able to get out of bed in order to wash in the bathroom, a pitcher of water and basin will be needed. If the patient is not able to wash, he or she may use dry cleansing, called *tayammum*. This is when a patient strikes the hands on a clean surface and then brushes his/her palms over the face and ears. A clean sheet will be needed to cover the body during prayer. For a male, from the waist down is required to be covered; for a female, the entire body, except for the face and hands, is required to be covered. Each of the prayers takes about five to ten minutes. All attention is given to God until the prayer is completed.

The seriously ill patient will find comfort in a companion who will read from the Qur'an, the sacred text of Islam.

Life is a gift from God that Muslims are expected to protect. It is "Allah Who gives you life, then gives you death" (Qur'an 45:26).[15] "It is Allah that takes the soul at death" (Qur'an 39:42).[16] Muslims are encouraged to prepare themselves for the hereafter by deeds and actions. This includes preparing wills and advanced directives.

Islam accepts the definition of brain dead as the definition for death. Brain dead is when the cortical and brainstem are no longer functioning.

Muslims are expected to render care for one another, especially the elderly. In protecting life, guiding principles are to advance the best efforts to maintain life and not to introduce unbearable pain or suffering. Hardship is considered a test from Allah. Patience, persistence, and hope are required of the family and friends. When there is no scientific hope of surviving the illness without extraordinary means, and no reasonable benefit to the patient, it is permissible to remove life-support equipment. The natural process of death then allows the dying person to accept the will of Allah.

Dying/Death

The body of the dying person should be on its side facing *Qiblah* (the wall that faces Mecca and the wall Muslims face when they pray). Friends and loved ones should pray that mercy, forgiveness, and blessings of Allah be given to the dying person. Friends and loved ones should read Surah 36 from the Qur'an—Surah Yaseen. People around the bedside should talk of the mercy, blessings, and forgiveness of Allah. The presence of loved ones and a religious leader at the bedside gives the dying person the opportunity to ask for forgiveness.

After death has occurred, a person of the same gender prepares the body for burial. Cremation is forbidden. Burial should occur the same day as death, if possible.

Prayers

For Any and Every Disease

O Allah, Lord of the people, remove all harm, give cure, for you are the one who cures. There is no curing except your curing—a curing that leaves no illness *(Bukhari)*.[17]

When an Illness Becomes Severe and One Is Overwhelmed

O Allah! Keep me alive as long as life is better for me and grant me death when death is better for me.[18]

During Distress

O Allah! Lord of Power (and Rule), Thou givest Power to whom Thou pleasest, and Thou strippest off Power from whom Thou pleasest: Thou enduest with honour whom Thou pleasest, and Thou bringest low whom Thou pleasest: in thy hand is all Good. Verily, over all things Thou hast power (Qur'an 3:26–27).[19]

For Perseverance

Our Lord! Pour out constancy on us and make our steps firm: help us against those that reject faith (Qur'an 2:250).[20]

For Protection and Mercy

O our Lord! Cover (us) with thy forgiveness—me, my parents, and (all) believers, on the Day that the Reckoning will be established! (Qur'an 14:41).[21]

For Seeking Pardon

O my Lord! I do seek refuge with Thee, lest I ask Thee for that of which I have no knowledge. And unless Thou forgive me and have Mercy on me, I should indeed be lost! (Qur'an 11:47).[22]

For Forgiveness

Our Lord! We have wronged our own souls: If Thou forgive us not and bestow not upon us Thy Mercy, we shall certainly be lost (Qur'an 7:23).[23]

For Victory against Odds

Our Lord! Pour out constancy on us and make our step firm: help us against those that reject faith (Qur'an 2:250).[24]

For Dying in Righteousness

O my Lord! Thou hast indeed bestowed on me some power, and taught me something of the interpretation of dreams and events—O thou creator of the heavens and the earth! Thou art my protector in this world and in the Hereafter. Take Thou my soul (at death) as one submitting to Thy will (as a Muslim), and unite me with the righteous (Qur'an 12:101).[25]

Remembering Those Who Have Died

To Allah we belong, and to Him is our return. They are those on whom (descend) blessings from their Lord, and Mercy, and they are the ones that receive guidance (Qur'an 2:156–157).[26]

Prayer for a Deceased Adult

O Allah, forgive our living and our deceased, our present and absent, our young and old, our men and women. O Allah, whomever You give life to, let him live on Islam and whomever You give death to, let him die on Iman *(Tirmidhi).*[27]

Prayer for a Deceased Child

O Allah, make this child a welcomer, forerunner, and a source of recompense for us *(Bukhari).*[28]

Jehovah's Witnesses

Beliefs

The name for God is *Jehovah* who is all-powerful, all knowing, and everlasting. Jehovah's Witnesses do not believe in the Trinity. Jesus is the first person of creation. The Holy Spirit is a force working for God. God, Jesus, and the Holy Spirit are three separate people. Satan is an enemy of God who leads people astray through temptation, nationalism, and spiritism. Man is born with sin because of the actions of Adam and Eve. When man dies, his soul dies as well. Heaven is the home of Jesus and the 144,000 people who gain access to heaven. Those who do not make it to heaven will disappear. There is no hell.

Jehovah's Witnesses do not celebrate Thanksgiving, Christmas, Easter, birthdays, or other holidays. The only day celebrated is the Memorial of Christ's death during the Passover.

Jehovah's Witnesses are required to learn the official doctrines, be willing to actively proselytize, participate in all congregational meetings, and be baptized into the faith.

Birth

There is no special ceremony at birth. Baptism occurs after much studying, as candidates for baptism must fully understand the doctrine of faith. A candidate for baptism attends several meetings where he or she is asked questions on the Bible, as well as historical and organizational questions. Answers are to be supported by giving specific references to the Bible and must be in agreement with the official doctrine of Jehovah's Witnesses. The actual baptism occurs at a large convention, which is held once or twice a year.

Diet

There are no dietary restrictions.

Sickness

Blood transfusions are not allowed. Organ transplants are a matter of individual conscience.

Dying/Death

No special requirements, except to respectfully care for the dying person and his or her family. And to respond to the individual needs of the patient and family.

Praying

If possible, one should pray with another Christian believer, for it says in Matthew 18:19: "If two of you agree on earth about anything you ask, it will be done for you by my Father in heaven."

Keep on praying in faith for your loved one. Perseverance produces results. Try not to be discouraged.

Pray by reading from the Bible, preferably the New World Translation.

Pray by speaking from your heart.

Judaism

Beliefs

There are three fundamental elements to religious Judaism: God, Torah, and Israel. It understands God to be a Creator, a Revealer, and a Redeemer. The Hebrew word *Torah* means "instruction," and refers to the first five books of the Bible. Jews have spoken of the *people* of Israel and of the *land* of Israel since biblical days. However, Jews are a people that transcend borders and races and cultural categorizations.[29]

There are four movements within Judaism: Orthodox, Reform, Conservative, and Reconstructionist. Most synagogues are affiliated with one of these movements. While the movements have different philosophies, members of these movements consider themselves to belong to the one Jewish people. Women in the Conservative, Reconstructionist, and Reform movements can be rabbis and cantors, and men and women sit together in synagogue. All movements recognize the centrality of God in their lives but have a different understanding of religious law *(Halahah)*.[30]

Birth

The Hebrew word for *"covenant"* is *Brit* and the ceremony for recognizing a male baby as being in the *Brit* is called *Brit Milah*, or "covenant of circumcision" as outlined in the Torah (Gen 17:9–14—24–25).[31] According to custom, circumcision takes place at the age of eight days, with the removal of the foreskin performed traditionally by the *mohel*, an individual specially trained in both the medical and ritual requirements of the procedure. At the *Brit* the baby boy receives his Hebrew name.

Jewish baby girls often receive their Hebrew name at the synagogue, usually within a month after birth. One custom is that the name is announced in connection with the father being called to the Torah during services. While Judaism does not have a specific ceremony similar to *Brit Milah*, Reform Judaism has instituted a ceremony for welcoming baby girls into the covenant called *Brit Ha-Chayim*, "covenant of life," or *Brit Bat*, "covenant of the daughter."[32]

Diet

The basis for kosher foods is the Bible (Lev 11:3–23; Deut 14:4–21), with the Talmudic teachings expanding the prohibitions: Beef, veal, and lamb, and the meat of chicken, ducks, geese, turkeys, and pigeons are kosher if slaughtered in the proper manner, and most other available meats are not. Only sea creatures with both fins and scales may be eaten, but shrimp, lobster, eels, shark, catfish, and shellfish are not. Meat and dairy products may not be eaten together.[33]

Individual Jews will vary widely in their observance of these dietary laws. Orthodox Jews eat kosher food in the home and also when eating in other places. Conservative Jews eat kosher food in the home, and will eat non-kosher fish or vegetables outside the home. Many Reform Jews in general do not "keep kosher."[34]

Fasting is done from sunset to one hour after sunset on the Day of Atonement, *Yom Kippur.* No food is eaten until after three stars are seen in the sky.

Sickness

In times of a serious illness, a Jewish person is not to be left alone. A family member is to be there with the person. It is the doctor's duty to prolong life. Doing anything that hastens the death of a dying person is not allowed. When death is imminent and certain, and the patient is suffering, a patient may refuse extraordinary means of prolonging life. Some branches of Judaism do not follow the Talmud strictly when it says they are "…not permitted to do anything that may hasten death, not even to prevent suffering."

Dying/Death

Jewish law opposes mutilation of the body and therefore autopsies are not permitted unless required by state law. An organ may be removed or donated only after the person is declared dead. However, the patient will need to be kept alive with the aid of a machine until the organ is retrieved. Orthodox Jews do not permit an autopsy or organ donations at all. For the same reasons cremation is forbidden.

From the moment of death until the funeral, the focus is on the deceased and the funeral. Tradition suggests that you not visit the family during this period. Jewish law provides that a funeral will take place within a day of death but never just before *Shabat* (i.e., Friday afternoon) or a holy day itself. A funeral may be delayed a day or two to allow relatives and friends from out of town to attend. Judaism does not have a wake.[35] Mourning takes place in the home after the funeral and lasts for seven days. This is to provide comfort to the family and show respect for the deceased.

When death occurs for an Orthodox Jew in a healthcare facility, the medical staff should make sure the arms are extended along the body and the fingers are outstretched. Tubing in the body is to remain and be clamped to the body. Body fluids are also to remain in the body. Any sheets, blankets, and the like, that have the patient's blood on them are to be kept with the patient and are to be buried with the body. A designated person of the Orthodox Jewish faith, familiar with Orthodox law, should clean the body. According to the Jewish tradition, someone is to be with the body reading prayers/psalms until the body is placed in the ground.

Prayers

The Road of Life

God of our life, there are days when our burdens overwhelm us, when the road ahead seems dreary, when the skies are gray and threatening. On such days our lives have no music, our hearts are lonely, and our spirits are robbed of courage. Flood our path with light, we beseech You; direct our vision to promising skies; attune our hearts to the uplifting music of life. Grant us the awareness of true comradeship with others, to sustain us, and so quicken our spirits that we may be able to encourage those who journey with us on the road of life to dedicate themselves to Your honor and glory. Amen.[36]

Prayer before an Operation

Heal us, O Lord, and we shall be healed, save us and we shall be saved; for You are our glory. Grant complete healing for all our afflictions, faithful and merciful God of healing.

Our Creator, who fashioned the human body with all its wonderful complexity, I turn to You in prayer. May the operation I am about to undergo help me return to health. Sustain the surgeon, the nurses, and attendants, instruments of Your healing power.

Strengthen, O God, my faith in You, so that I may face this ordeal with serenity and with fortitude. Amen.[37]

Prayer for the Sick and Wounded

Blessed art Thou, O Lord our God, [Ruler] of the universe, who grantest blessings on the undeserving, for on me hast Thou bestowed good favor.

A prayer of the afflicted, when he is downcast, and pours out his complaint before the Lord: O Lord, hear my prayer, and let my cry come unto Thee. Hide not Thy face from me in the day of my distress; incline Thine ear unto me; in the day when I call answer me speedily. I beseech Thee, O Lord, healer of all flesh, have mercy upon me, and support me in Thy grace upon my bed of sickness, for I am weak. Send relief and cure to me and to all that are sick among Thy children. Soothe my pain, and renew my youth as the eagle's. Grant wisdom unto the physician that he may cure my wound, so that my health may be restored speedily. Hear my prayer, prolong my life, let me complete my tears in happiness, that I may be enabled to serve Thee and keep Thy statutes with a perfect heart. Give me understanding to know that this bitter trial has come upon me for my welfare, so that I may not despise Thy discipline, nor weary of Thy reproof.

O God of forgiveness, who art gracious and merciful, slow to anger and abounding in loving kindness, I confess unto Thee with a broken and contrite heart that I have sinned, and have done that which is evil in

Thy sight. Behold, I repent of my evil way, and return unto Thee with perfect repentance. Help me, O God of my salvation, that I may not again turn unto folly, but walk before Thee in truth and uprightness. Rejoice the soul of Thy servant, for unto Thee, O Lord, do I lift my soul. Heal me, O Lord, and I shall be healed, save me, and I shall be saved, for Thou art my praise. Amen. Amen![38]

Prayer on Recovery from Sickness

Blessed art Thou, O Lord our God, [Ruler] of the universe, who grantest blessings on the undeserving, for on me hast Thou bestowed good favor.

O God, great, mighty, and revered, in the abundance of Thy loving kindness I come before Thee to render thanks for all the benefits Thou hast bestowed upon me. In my distress I called upon Thee, and Thou hast answered me; from my bed of pain I cried unto Thee, and Thou hast heard the voice of my supplication. Thou hast sorely chastened me, O Lord, but Thou hast not given me over unto death. In Thy love and pity Thou broughtest up my soul from the grave. For Thine anger is but for a moment; Thy favor is for a lifetime: weeping may tarry for the night, but joy comes in the morning. Yea, the living, he shall praise Thee, as I do this day, and my soul that Thou hast redeemed shall tell Thy wonders unto the children of men. Blessed art Thou, the faithful physician unto all flesh.

O God, merciful and gracious, who dispenses kindness to the undeserving, I am indeed unworthy of all the mercies Thou hast hitherto shown unto me. O purify my heart, that I may be fitted to walk in the way of the upright before Thee; and continue Thy help unto Thy servant. Restore me to perfect health, and with bodily vigor bless Thou me. Remove from me all sorrow and care, preserve me from all evil, and guide me with Thine own counsel; so shall the sun of righteousness ever rise unto me with healing in its wings.

Let the words of my mouth and the meditation of my heart be acceptable before Thee, O Lord, my Rock and my Redeemer. Amen.[39]

Appropriate Prayers for the Sick

Psalms 20, 23, 79, 91, and 123.

Shema Yisroel Adoni Alohaynu Adonoi Ehod. Hear, O Israel, the Lord is our God, the Lord is One (Deut 6:4).

Psalm 143

Hashem, hear my prayer, listen to my supplication, answer me in Your faithfulness, in Your righteousness. And do not enter into strict judgment with Your servant, for no living creature would be innocent before You. For the enemy pursued my soul, he ground my life into the dirt, he sat me in utter darkness, like those who are long dead. When my spirit grew faint upon me, within me my heart was appalled; I recalled days of old; I pondered over all Your deeds; I spoke about Your handiwork. I spread out my hands to You, my soul longs for You like the thirsty land. Selah answer me soon, O Hashem, my spirit is spent; conceal not Your face from me, lest I be like those who descend into the pit. Let me hear Your kindness at dawn, for in You have I placed my trust; let me know the way I should walk, for to You have I lifted my soul. Rescue me from my enemies, Hashem, I have hidden my plight from all but You. Teach me to do Your will, for You are my God. May Your good spirit guide me over level ground. For Your Name's sake, Hashem, revive me, with Your righteousness remove my soul from distress. And with Your kindness cut off my enemies; and destroy all who oppress my soul, for I am Your servant.[40]

Av Ha-Rachameem — Theme of Grief

Compassionate Father who dwells on high, in His powerful compassion may he remember with compassion the devout, the upright, and the blameless ones, the holy communities who gave their lives for the sanctification of the Divine Name. Those who were beloved and pleasant in their lifetime were not parted in their death. They were quicker than eagles and stronger than lions to do the will of their Creator's will and the wish of their Rock.

41

May our God remember them for good with the other righteous of the world. May He bring retribution before our eyes for the spilled blood of His servants. As is written in the Torah of Moses, the man of God, "Sing aloud, nations of His people, because He will avenge the blood of His servants and He will bring retribution on His adversaries; and He will expiate His land and His people" (Deut 32:43).

And by the hands of Your servants, the prophets, is written saying, "Though I cleanse, their bloodshed I will not cleanse when God dwells in Zion" (Joel 4:21).

And in the Holy Writings it is said, "Why should the nations say, 'Where is their God?' Let it be known among nations, before our eyes, the avenging of Your servants' spilled blood" (Ps 79:10).

And it says "For the Avenger of blood has remembered them; he has not forgotten the cry of the humble" (Ps 9:13). And it says, "He will judge the nations filled with corpses, he will crush the head of the large land. From a river along the way he shall drink, therefore he may lift up his head" (Ps 110:6–7).[41]

Confessional on the Death Bed

I acknowledge before You, Hashem, my God and the God of my forefathers, that my recovery and death are in Your hand. May it be Your will You heal me with total recovery, but, if I die, may my death be an atonement for all the errors, iniquities, and willful sins that I have erred, sinned, and transgressed before You. You grant my share in the Garden of Eden, and privilege me for the World to Come that is concealed for the righteous.[42]

Words Spoken at a Jewish Funeral

Adonai natan, adonai, y'hi shem adonai m'vorach. (God has given and God has taken away. Blessed be the name of the Lord.)[43]

Memorial Prayer

God full of mercy who dwells on high, grant perfect rest on the wings of Your Divine Presence. In the lofty heights of the holy and pure who shine as the brightness of the heavens to the soul of (person's name) who has gone to his eternal rest as all his family and friends pray for the elevation of his soul, his resting place shall be in the Garden of Eden. Therefore, the Master of mercy will care for him under the protection of His wings for all time. And bind his soul in the bond of everlasting life. God is his inheritance and he will rest in peace, and let us say Amen.[44]

Orthodox Christianity

Beliefs

The Orthodox Church is a communion of self-governing churches that are united by a common faith and spirituality. Administratively independent, they are all in communion with the Ecumenical Patriarch of Constantinople. Orthodox Christians share similar beliefs with Roman Catholics, and have a similar creed believing in Jesus Christ, his death and resurrection, and the Holy Trinity. Mary the Mother of Jesus is highly honored in the Orthodox Church. However, the immaculate conception is not a teaching or a dogma. They teach that Mary was fully human, and that after her death, rather than ascending into heaven, she was buried like all humans.

An Orthodox Christian may go to any Orthodox Church and receive the sacraments: Baptism, Chrismation (Confirmation), Holy Communion, Confession, Anointing of the Sick (Holy Unction), Matrimony, and Holy Orders. With the exception of Holy Orders, the sacraments can be performed by an Orthodox priest. The Bible, both Old and New Testaments, and Holy Tradition are the sources of belief.

Birth

Holy Baptism is performed any time after the Fortieth Day Blessing, when parents bring the infant to church for the first time. At baptism, three sacraments take place: Holy Baptism, which is celebrated by three-fold immersion in the name of the Trinity; Holy Chrismation; and Holy Communion. The infant is considered a full member of the Church. In cases of emergency, when an infant may be dying, anyone—male or female—who believes in the Holy Trinity, can perform what is known as the baptism of air: lifting the child in the air and saying: "The servant of God is baptized in the name of the Father, the Son, and the Holy Spirit." If the child survives, then he or she is brought to the church for Chrismation and Holy Communion. Holy Confession is received as an adult.

Diet

Abstinence means no milk, eggs, fish, or meat. Abstinence is observed on every Wednesday and Friday, and every day during the Great Lent (50 days leading to Easter), and all fasts. Fasts days are: the 25 days prior to Christmas; "3 days" Lent (Triduum); the Great Lent, 13 days prior to the Festival of St. Peter and St. Paul; and 15 days prior to the Dormition (Falling Asleep) of the Virgin Mary (August 15). Exceptions: Milk and fish may be consumed by those who choose on Wednesdays and Fridays, except during the Lent times.

While fasting is required on the "3 days" Lent and all the days of the Great Lent except Saturdays and Sundays, people are encouraged to eat in moderation at all times.

The very sick are not expected to observe fasting, although they should not eat just prior to receiving Holy Communion.

Sickness

The Orthodox Church opposes euthanasia. The Church does approve of the use of drugs to reduce pain and suffering. In the case where death is unavoidable and the person is spiritually prepared for death by confession and communion, the Church does not interfere with the use of life-support machines/drugs. Removing life-support machines/drugs should be done after prayer, as well as discussion with family members, a medical professional, and a spiritual director.

Organ donation is an acceptable practice, because an Orthodox Christian dies believing what the Lord has said: "Greater love hath no man than this, that a man lay down his life for his friends" (John 15:13).[45]

Dying/Death

As a loved one dies, the family is encouraged to be at the bedside, along with other close friends, and to invite a priest to be present. For a prolonged illness, prayers are said at the bedside to ask God to let his servant go in peace. A priest should conduct the sacrament of the Anointing of the Sick (Holy Unction) using blessed oil.

An Orthodox Christian must have the body buried in the ground. Burial must include a coffin, a grave or cemetery plot with a grave liner, and a grave monument that includes an image of the cross. Because the Orthodox faith affirms the fundamental goodness of creation, it understands the body to be an integral part of the human person and the temple of the Holy Spirit, and expects the resurrection of the dead. Therefore, cremation is not allowed, and the Church does not grant funerals to persons who have chosen to be cremated.

Prayers

Prayer to the Holy Spirit

O Heavenly King, the comforter, the spirit of Truth, Who art present everywhere and fillest all things; Treasury of Blessings and Giver of Life; come and abide in us and cleanse us from every stain, and save our souls, O Gracious One.[46]

Prayers of Thanksgiving

O Lord my Savior and my Master, I, Thine unprofitable servant, with fear and trembling give thanks unto Thy loving goodness for all Thy benefits which Thou hast poured so abundantly upon me, Thy servant. I fall down in adoration before Thee and offer Thee, O God, my praises; with fervor I cry to Thee: O God, deliver henceforth from all adversities and mercifully fulfill in me such of my desires as may be expedient for me. Hear me, I entreat Thee, and have mercy, for Thou art the Hope of all the ends of the earth, and unto Thee, with the Father, and the Holy Spirit, be ascribed glory, now and ever, and unto ages of ages. Amen.[47]

I praise Thee, O God of our Fathers, I hymn Thee, I bless Thee, I give thanks unto Thee for Thy great and tender mercy. To Thee I flee, O merciful and mighty God. Shine into my heart with the True Sun of Thy righteousness. Enlighten my mind and keep all my senses, that henceforth I may walk uprightly and keep Thy commandments, and may finally attain unto eternal life, even to Thee, Who art the source of life, and be admitted to the glorious fruition of Thy inaccessible Light. For Thou art my God, and unto Thee, O Father, Son and Holy Spirit, be ascribed glory, now and ever and unto ages of ages. Amen.[48]

Lord, I Have Cried to You

Lord, I have cried out to You; hear me! Hear me, O Lord! Lord, I have cried out unto You: hear me! Receive the voice of my prayers! When I call upon

You, hear me, O Lord! Let my prayer arise in Your sight as incense, and let the lifting up of my hands be an evening sacrifice. Hear me, O Lord![49]

Psalm 3

LORD, how are they increased that trouble me!
    Many are they that rise up against me.
Many there be which say of my soul,
    There is no help for him in God.

But thou, O LORD, art a shield for me;
    my glory, and the lifter up of mine head.
I cried unto the LORD with my voice,
    and he heard me out of his holy hill.

I laid me down and slept;
    I awaked; for the LORD sustained me.
I will not be afraid of ten thousands of people,
    that have set themselves against me round about.

Arise, O LORD;
    save me, O my God:
for thou hast smitten all mine enemies upon the
      cheek bone;
    thou hast broken the teeth of the ungodly.

Salvation belongeth unto the LORD:
    thy blessing is upon thy people.[50]

Psalm 23

The LORD is my shepherd; I shall not want.
  He maketh me to lie down in green pastures:
he leadeth me beside the still waters.
  He restoreth my soul:
he leadeth me in the paths of righteousness
  for his name's sake.

Yea, though I walk through the valley of the shadow
    of death,
  I will fear no evil:
for thou art with me;
  thy rod and thy staff
  they comfort me.

Thou preparest a table before me
  in the presence of mine enemies:
thou anointest my head with oil;
  my cup runneth over.
Surely goodness and mercy shall follow me
  all the days of my life:
and I will dwell in the house of the LORD for ever.[51]

Prayers Near Death When a Priest Is Not Available

O Lord, visit in your grace those in afflictions, heal the
sick in your mercy and console the sorrowful in your
compassion. Grant health to the body, mind, and soul

of those who thirst for your mercy and kindness, especially this your servant who is sick, in order that we may thank you, Father, Son and Holy Spirit, now and always and for ever and ever. Amen.

Glory be to you O Lord, who visits the weak souls, who scrutinizes the hidden things, who answers the worthy petitions, who gives consolation to the mourners and encouragement to the sorrowful, who supports the weak, who heals the sick, who accepts the penitents making them His disciples, and who raises the dead. We plead for the remission of debts and forgiveness of sins, for us and those who have asked for our intercessions. May we offer honor, adoration, and praise to you now at this time.

O Lord our God, you are the real and perfect physician. All the hidden and visible pains of the body, mind, and soul are easy before you. We now pray for your servant who is in weakness, who has fallen into sickness, who is seeking your mercy, who is craving for your gift of help and who is praying for the remission of debts, the forgiveness of sins and the healing of diseases and for health. O merciful Lord, you strengthen the weak and forgive the sinners. You are the helper of the penitents, the strength of those in trouble and the refuge of all the faithful. Remit this servant's debts and forgive his/her sins. Remove his/her pains and heal his/her illness. Cast away all his/her afflictions. Be a support to his/her weakness. Strengthen him/her in his/her trials. Remove his/her disappointment and gladden us through his/her recovery. May he/she rise up and offer thanks for your grace and help. You are the perfect one, merciful and kind, and full of grace. You are the real physician of the body, mind, and soul. O God the Father, you are worthy of praise, honor, and dominion along with your only-begotten Son and the Holy Spirit, now and always and for ever and ever. Amen.[52]

Prayer When a Child Dies

O Lord who watches over children in the present life and in the world to come because of their simplicity and innocence of mind, abundantly satisfying them with a place in Abraham's bosom, bringing them to live in radiantly shining places where the spirits of the righteous dwell: receive in peace the soul of Your little servant (name), for You Yourself have said, "Let the little children come to Me, for such is the Kingdom of Heaven." Amen.[53]

Roman Catholicism

Beliefs

Roman Catholics are Christians and believe that Jesus Christ is the Son of God, who was born of the Virgin Mary, died on the cross, and rose from the dead. Jesus is the second person of the Trinity. The Trinity is God in three persons: Father, Son, and Holy Spirit. Catholics believe they need to know, love, and serve God in order to enter eternal happiness, which is ultimately reached through the grace of God.

While Roman Catholics observe the Ten Commandments, the two greatest that Jesus taught are to "Love the Lord your God with all your heart and with all your soul and with all your strength and with all your mind" and "Love your neighbor as yourself" (Luke 10:27). The laws of the church include: attending Mass on Sunday; receiving the Eucharist during the Easter season; receiving the sacrament of reconciliation at least once a year; fasting and abstaining on the required days; and contributing to the support of the church.

Birth

Catholics believe children are born with original sin as the result of the disobedience of Adam and Eve to God. The sacrament of baptism washes away this sin and initiates the person into the Catholic community. During the ceremony, parents and godparents promise to teach the child about their faith. The child will receive a candle representing the light of Christ that has entered his/her life, and a white robe symbolic of the new life in Christ. While a child is usually named at birth, it is at baptism that a person is formally given a Christian name and becomes a member of the Roman Catholic Church.

Diet

Catholics fast on Ash Wednesday, the Fridays of Lent, and Good Friday. In addition, from the age of fourteen to fifty-nine, Catholics abstain from meat and meat products on Ash Wednesday and Good Friday.

In addition, Catholics are to fast for an hour before receiving the Eucharist. However, this is not strictly enforced for patients in a hospital.

Sickness

A person has a moral obligation to use ordinary or proportionate means of preserving life. A person may forgo extraordinary or disproportionate means of preserving life. Proportionate here is in the judgment of the patient, where the treatment offers reasonable benefit and does not entail excessive burden or expense on the family.[54]

Dying/Death

According to the Letter of James (5:14), if you are sick you should pray and be anointed with oil in the name of the Lord. The sacrament of the anointing of the sick should be administered to anyone with a serious illness, before a major operation, to the elderly if their condition has weakened, and to a child if they can be strengthened by the sacrament. The sacrament can be administered to someone who is unconscious if, while they were conscious, they would have desired the sacrament. Once the person has died, the sacrament may not be administered. The anointing of the sick can only be ministered by a priest.[55]

Funeral arrangements may include the option of cremation. Cremated remains may be brought to the Funeral Mass if cremation takes place before the Funeral Rite.[56]

Prayers

Our Father

Our Father, who art in heaven, hallowed be Thy name; Thy kingdom come; Thy will be done, on earth as it is in heaven. Give us this day our daily bread; and forgive us our trespasses as we forgive those who trespass against us; and lead us not into temptation, but deliver us from evil. Amen.

Hail Mary

Hail Mary, full of grace, the Lord is with thee; blessed art Thou among women; and blessed is the fruit of Thy womb, Jesus. Holy Mary, Mother of God, pray for us sinners, now and at the hour of our death. Amen.

Glory Be to the Father

Glory be to the Father, and to the Son, and to the Holy Spirit; as it was in the beginning, is now, and ever shall be, world without end. Amen.

Act of Contrition

I confess to almighty God, and to you, my brothers and sisters, that I have sinned through my own fault, in my thoughts and in my words, in what I have done, and in what I have failed to do; and I ask blessed Mary, ever virgin, all the angels and saints, and you, my brothers and sisters, to pray for me to the Lord our God. May almighty God have mercy on us, forgive us our sins, and bring us to everlasting life. Amen.

Prayer for the Sick

Watch, O Lord, with those who wake, or watch, or weep tonight, and give your angels charge over those who sleep.

Tend your sick ones, O Lord Christ.
Rest your weary ones.
Bless your dying ones.
Soothe your suffering ones.
Pity your afflicted ones.
Shield your joyous ones.
And for all your love's sake. Amen[57]

—Saint Augustine

Psalm 121

I lift up my eyes to the hills—
    where does my help come from?
My help comes from the LORD,
    the Maker of heaven and earth.

He will not let your foot slip—
    he who watches over you will not slumber;
indeed, he who watches over Israel
    will neither slumber nor sleep.

The LORD watches over you—
    the LORD is your shade at your right hand;

the sun will not harm you by day,
nor the moon by night.

The LORD will keep you from all harm—
he will watch over your life;
the LORD will watch over
your coming and going
both now and forevermore.

Psalm for the Sick

O Lord, in your anger punish me not; in your wrath chastise me not. For your arrows have sunk deep in me; your hand has come down upon me. There is no health in my flesh because of your indignation; there is no wholeness in my bones because of my sin. For my iniquities have overwhelmed me; they are like a heavy burden, beyond my strength. Noisome and festering are my sores, because of my folly. I am stooped and bowed down profoundly; all the day I go in mourning. For my loins are filled with burning pains; there is no health in my flesh. I am numbed and severely crushed; I roar with anguish of heart. O Lord, all my desire is before you; from you my groaning is not hid. My heart throbs, my strength forsakes me; the very light of my eyes has failed me. For I am very near to falling; and my grief is with me always. Indeed, I acknowledge my guilt; I grieve over my sins. Forsake me not, O Lord; my God be not far from me! Make haste to help me, O Lord, my salvation. Let me know, O Lord, my end and what is the number of my days, that I may learn how frail I am. A short span you have made my days, and my life is as nought before you; only a breath is any human existence. Hear my prayer, O Lord, to my cry give ear; to my weeping be not deaf! For I am but a wayfarer before you, a pilgrim like all my fathers. Turn your gaze from me that I may find respite, ere I depart and be no more.[58] (Taken from Psalms 37 and 38.)

Prayers for Healing

Lord, You invite all who are burdened to come to You. Allow your healing hand to heal me. Touch my soul with Your compassion for others. Touch my heart with Your courage and infinite love for all. Touch my mind with Your wisdom, that my mouth may always proclaim Your praise. Teach me to reach out to You in my need, and help me to lead others to You by my example. Most loving Heart of Jesus, bring me health in body and spirit that I may serve You with all my strength. Touch gently this life which You have created, now and forever. Amen.[59]

Lord, look upon me with eyes of mercy, may your healing hand rest upon me, may your life-giving powers flow into every cell of my body and into the depths of my soul, cleansing, purifying, restoring me to wholeness and strength for service in your Kingdom. Amen.[60]

O God who are the only source of health and healing, the spirit of calm and the central peace of this universe, grant to me such a consciousness of your indwelling and surrounding presence that I may permit you to give me health and strength and peace, through Jesus Christ our Lord. Amen.[61]

Prayer before Surgery

Loving Father, I entrust myself to your care this day. Guide with wisdom and skill the minds and hands of the medical people who minister in your Name, and grant that every cause of illness be removed, that I may be restored to soundness of health and learn to live in more perfect harmony with you and with those around me. Through Jesus Christ. Amen.[62]

Prayer after Surgery

Blessed Savior, I thank you that this operation is safely past, and now I rest in your abiding presence, relaxing every tension, releasing every care and anxiety, receiving more and more of your healing life into every part of my being. In moments of pain I turn to you for strength, in times of loneliness I feel your loving nearness. Grant that your life and love and joy may flow through me for the healing of others in your name. Amen.[63]

Prayer for Doctors and Nurses

O merciful Father, who have wonderfully fashioned man in your own image, and made his body to be a temple of the Holy Spirit, sanctify, we pray you, our doctors and nurses and all those whom you have called to study and practice the arts of healing the sick and the prevention of disease and pain. Strengthen them in body and soul, and bless their work, that they may give comfort to those for whose salvation your Son became Man, lived on this earth, healed the sick, and suffered and died on the Cross. Amen.[64]

Prayer of Thanksgiving

Thank you, O God, for hearing my prayer and granting my request. Thank you for all the kindness you have shown me. Thank you, Father, for your great love in giving me my life, for your great patience in preserving me despite my sinfulness, for your protection in the past and for the opportunity to serve and honor you in the future. Thank you, Lord Jesus, for keeping me numberless times from sin and death by the toils of your life, the sufferings of your Passion, and by your victorious Resurrection. Thank you, Holy Spirit of God, for bestowing so many graces upon my soul and for having so frequently renewed your life within me. May my life, from now on, be a sign of my gratefulness. Amen.[65]

Litany at the Hour of Death

Holy Mary, Mother of God	Pray for him/her
Holy Angels of God	Pray for him/her
Saint John the Baptist	Pray for him/her
Saint Joseph	Pray for him/her
Saint Peter and Saint Paul	Pray for him/her
All holy men and women	Pray for him/her

I commend you, my dear brother/sister,
    to almighty God,
and entrust you to your Creator.
May you return to him
who formed you from the dust of the earth.
May holy Mary, the angels, and all the saints
come to meet you as you go forth from this life.
May Christ who was crucified for you
bring you freedom and peace.
May Christ who died for you
admit you into his garden of paradise.
May Christ, the true Shepherd,
acknowledge you as one of his flock.
May he forgive all your sins,
and set you among those he has chosen.
May you see your Redeemer face to face,
and enjoy the vision of God for ever.

R. Amen.[66]

Prayer after Death

Holy Lord, almighty and eternal God,
hear our prayers for your servant N.,
whom you have summoned out of this world.
Forgive his/her sins and failings
and grant him/her a place of refreshment, light,
    and peace.
Let him/her pass unharmed through the gates
    of death
to dwell with the blessed in light,
as you promised to Abraham and his children forever.
Accept N. into your safekeeping
and on the great day of judgment
raise him/her with all the saints
to inherit your eternal kingdom.

We ask this through Christ our Lord.

R. Amen.[67]

For Those Who Mourn

Father of mercies and God of all consolation,
you pursue us with untiring love
and dispel the shadow of death
with the bright dawn of life.

[Comfort your family in their loss and sorrow.
Be our refuge and our strength, O Lord,

and lift us from the depths of grief
into the peace and light of your presence.]

Your Son, our Lord Jesus Christ,
by dying has destroyed our death,
and by rising, restored our life.
Enable us therefore to press on toward him,
so that, after our earthly course is run,
he may reunite us with those we love,
when every tear will be wiped away.

We ask this through Christ our Lord.

R. Amen.[68]

For All Faiths

A Prayer for Servicemen and Servicewomen

Lord, you have called all of us to serve one another in humility and truth. Help our men and women in military service to remain steadfast in all efforts to assist the cause of peace and justice throughout the world.

Fill them with the strength and grace to be true
    peacemakers;
fill them with the courage to follow their consciences
    and your will in all things.
Keep them safe.
Guide and protect them always.
Stand by them always.
Stand by them whether they are home or away from
    home,
that they may always find you near,
and that they may always remain near to you.
I ask this in your name, Lord Jesus. Amen. [69]

Notes

1. Father Mychal Judge, OFM, Holy Name Province, Order of Friars Minor—Franciscan Friars, New York.

2. Francesa Fremantle and Chogyam Trungpa, *Tibetan Book of the Dead* (Boston: Shambhala, 1975).

3. Reprinted from *Occasional Services: A Companion to Lutheran Book of Worship* (Minneapolis, MN: Augsburg Fortress Publishers, 1982).

4. Holy Bible, New Living Translation (Wheaton, IL: Tyndale House Publishers, Inc., 1996). Adapted by Sing Cher Kwek. Singapore. http://www.inspiringword. net/movies/psa-23a.htm

5. The World Prayers Project, http://www.world prayers.org. The original source is unknown.

6. http://1stholistic.com/Spl_prayers/prayer _maha-mantra.htm (Akron, OH: International Cyber Business Services, Inc., 1998, 2004).

7. Ibid.

8. Ibid.

9. Ibid.

10. Ibid.

11. Ibid.

12. Ibid.

13. Rabbi Marc Gellman and Msgr. Thomas Hartman, *Religion for Dummies* (New York: Wiley Publishing, Inc., 2002), 366.

14. Ibid., 159.

15. Abdullah Yusuf Ali, *The Meaning of the Holy Qur'ān* (Beltsville, MD: Amana Publications, 2004).

16. Ibid.

17. *Summarized—Sahih-Al Bukhan Hadith* (Corona, Elmhurst, Queens, NY: Dar-us-Salam Publisher, 1994). Please note: *Bukhari* and *Tirmidhi* are both in the *Hadith* (Sayings of the Prophet Mohammed).

18. Ibid.

19. Abdullah Yusuf Ali, *The Meaning of the Holy Qur'ān.*

20. Ibid.

21. Ibid.

22. Ibid.

23. Ibid.

24. Ibid.

25. Ibid.

26. Ibid.

27. *Summarized—Sahih-Al Bukhan Hadith.*

28. Ibid.

29. Michael Lotker, *A Christian's Guide to Judaism* (Mahwah, NJ: Paulist Press, 2004), 8.

30. Ibid., 6–7.

31. Ibid., 66–67.

32. Ibid.

33. Ibid., 87–88.

34. Ibid.

35. Ibid., 68–69.

36. Source Unknown.

37. Rabbi Nossan Scherman, and Rabbi Meir Zlotowitz, eds., *The Complete Art Scroll Siddur* (Prayer Book) (Brooklyn, NY: Artscroll/Mesorah Publications, Ltd.), 799.

38. Ibid.

39. Ibid.

40. Ibid.

41. Ibid.

42. Ibid.

43. Ibid.

44. Ibid.

45. Scripture taken from the King James Version of the Bible (Wheaton, IL: Tyndale House Publishers, 1987).

46. http://www.ocf.org/Orthodox Page/prayers. A prayer used for centuries by the Greek Orthodox Church. Original source unknown.

47. Ibid.

48. Ibid.

49. Standard Prayer from the Vespers Service, Greek Orthodox Church. Reprinted from http://www.goarch.org/en/resources/prayers.

50. King James Version of the Bible.

51. Ibid.

52. Mathews Mar Barnabas, *Handbook for the Malankara Orthodox* (The Malankara Orthodox Syrian Church, Bellrose, NY, 1995). Standard Prayer from the Vespers Service, Greek Orthodox Church. Reprinted from http://www.goarch.org/en/resources/prayers.

53. http://www.transchurch.org/sguide/praybk.htm

54. United States Conference of Catholic Bishops, *Ethical and Religious Directives for Catholic Health Care Services*, Directives 56, 57, p. 31.

55. United States Conference of Catholic Bishops, *Pastoral Care of the Sick: Rites of Anointing and Viaticum* (New York: Catholic Book Publishing Co., 1983), 8–16.

56. United States Conference of Catholic Bishops, *Order of Christian Funerals* (Totowa, NJ: Catholic Book Publishing Co., 1998), #413, p. 391; #426–427, p. 393–394.

57. http://www.catholic.org/clife/prayers. Catholic Online, Bakersfield, CA.

58. Ibid.

59. Ibid.

60. Ibid.

61. Ibid.

62. Ibid.

63. Ibid.

64. Ibid.

65. United States Conference of Catholic Bishops, A *Ritual for Laypersons* (Collegeville, MN: The Liturgical Press, 1993), 85–86, 91, 93; excerpts from the English translation of *Pastoral Care of the Sick: Rites of Anointing and Viaticum*, ICEL, 1982; excerpts from the *Order of Christian Funerals*, ICEL, 1985. All rights reserved.

66. Ibid.

67. Ibid.

68. William H. Woestman, *The Shrine Prayer Book* (Belleville, IL: Shrine of Our Lady of the Snows, 1973).

69. Ibid. Adapted.

References

Ali, Abdullah Yusuf, *The Meaning of the Holy Qur'ān* (11th edition). Beltsville, MD: Amana Publications, 2004.

Barnabas, Mathews Mar, *Handbook for the Malankara Orthodox.* Bellrose, NY: The Malankara Orthodox Syrian Church, 1995.

Fremantle, Francesca, and Chogyam Trungpa, *Tibetan Book of the Dead.* Boston: Shambhala, 1975.

Gellman, Rabbi Marc, and Msgr. Thomas Hartman, *How Do You Spell God?* New York: Morrow Junior Books, 1995.

Gellman, Rabbi Marc, and Msgr. Thomas Hartman, *Religion for Dummies.* New York: Wiley Publishing, Inc., 2002.

Holy Bible, New International Version. Grand Rapids, MI: Zondervan, 1973, 1978, 1984.

Holy Bible, New Living Translation. Wheaton, IL: Tyndale House Publishers, 1996.

King James Version of the Bible. Wheaton, IL: Tyndale House Publishers, 1987.

Kirkwood, Neville A., *A Hospital Handbook on Multiculturalism and Religion.* Harrisburg, PA: Morehouse Publishing, 1993.

Lotker, Michael, *A Christian's Guide to Judaism*. Mahwah, NJ: Paulist Press, 2004.

Occasional Services: A Companion to Lutheran Book of Worship. Minneapolis, MN: Augsburg Fortress, 1982.

Rinpoche, Sogyal, *The Tibetan Book of Living and Dying*. San Francisco: Harper San Francisco, 1992.

Scherman, Rabbi Nosson, and Rabbi Meir Zlotowitz, eds. *The Complete Art Scroll Siddur*. New York: Artscroll/Mesorah Publications, Ltd., 1984.

Summarized—Sahih-Al Bukhan Hadith. Queens, NY: Dar-us-Salem Publisher, 1994.

Transfiguration Orthodox Prayer Book. Compiled from various sources by Fr. Peter Gregory. http://www. transchurch.org/sguide/praybk.htm

United States Conference of Catholic Bishops, *A Ritual for Laypersons*. Collegeville, MN: The Liturgical Press, 1993.

United States Conference of Catholic Bishops, *Ethical and Religious Directives for Catholic Health Care Services*, Fourth Edition, Directives 56, 57. Washington, D.C.: USCCB, 2001.

United States Conference of Catholic Bishops, *Pastoral Care of the Sick: Rites of Anointing and Viaticum*, New York: Catholic Book Publishing Co., 1983.

United States Conference of Catholic Bishops, *Order of Christian Funerals*, Totowa, NJ: Catholic Book Publishing Co., 1998.

Woestman, William H., *The Shrine Prayer Book*. Belleville, IL: Shrine of Our Lady of the Snows, 1973.

Websites

http://1stholistic.com/spl_prayers/prayer_maha-mantra.htm
http://home.it.net.au/~jgrapsas/pages/euthanasia.htm
http://islam.about.com/blhealth1/htm
http://mferguson76.com/a_jw.html
http://www.beliefnet.com/story/26/story_2656.html
http://www.catholic.org/clife/prayers
http://www.geocities.com/Tokyo/Dojo/1299/buddha.htm
http://www.ggalanti.com/cultural_profiles/eastindian.html
http://www.goarch.org/en/resources/prayers/psalms/psalm_3.asp
http://www.hindunet.org/samskars/index.htm
http://www.holy-trinity.org/liturgics/sokolov-death.html
http://www.inspiringword.net/movies/psa-23a.htm
http://www.jewfaq.org/death.htm
http://www.jewishfuneralcare.com/prayers.shtml
http://www.ocf.org/orthodoxpage/intro.html
http://www.themodernreligion.com/death/recommendations.html
http://www.transchurch.org/sguide/praybk.htm
http://www.watchtowerinformationservice.org/jws.htm
http://www.worldprayers.org

Compassionate Care

He who began a good work in you
will carry it on to completion
until the day of Christ Jesus. (Philippians 1:6)